OPEN
TO THE
SOURCE

OPEN
TO THE
SOURCE

SELECTED TEACHINGS OF
Douglas E. Harding

EDITED BY
Richard Lang

INNER DIRECTIONS®
The Spirit of Insight & Awakening

Inner Directions ®

INNER DIRECTIONS FOUNDATION
P.O. Box 130070
Carlsbad, California 92013
Tel: 800 545-9118 • 760 599-4075
www.InnerDirections.org

Cover and interior design by Joan Greenblatt
Printed in Canada on recycled paper

ISBN-10: 1-878019-23-6
ISBN-13: 978-1-878019-23-3

Library of Congress Catalog Card Number: 2005929160

For my

mother and father,

my sister and brother.

If you really want
to live the aware
life, to wake up
from the social
dream, to be
Who you are,
everything will
spring to your
aid and push
you towards
that supreme
goal.

TABLE OF CONTENTS

TEN EXPERIMENTS

INTRODUCTION

Douglas Harding is a highly regarded philosopher, spiritual teacher, and the author of many books. He has developed a unique way of awakening to the Source, of seeing Who we really are. His approach, which is original, effective, direct, and practical, goes right to the Heart of the matter, guiding us straight home to our True Nature, our Divinity.

Thoroughly versed in the writings of the world's great mystics, Harding is deeply traditional. His distinctive voice lies wholly within the long spiritual tradition that stretches from the ancient Indian Upanishads through the seers of all the great religions to the present day. Yet Harding's method of awakening is primarily inspired by modern science. It appeals to the evidence of the senses rather than on revealed truth.

Accordingly, respectful as Harding is of the great mystics, the starting point of this Way is no sacred text but your unmediated experience of yourself. What are you here and now? Who are you really? Harding points to the observable fact that what you are at center is completely different from what you are from a distance. Are you *essentially* a "thing," separate from other things, or are you No-thing, which is *capacity* for things?

The point is to put aside what others say and look for yourself. A central refrain of Harding's is that you are the sole and final authority on you. Delegate to no one the power to decide who you really are. Harding applies this rule to his own teaching: "Don't believe a word I say! Test it!"

At the heart of this contemporary path home to your Self are the *experiments*. Developed by Harding, these unique awareness exercises are important, indeed vital, because they provide directions so easy and so straightforward that you can see the Source in a moment—if you're willing to look in the right place with an open mind. It doesn't matter if you've never done anything like this before, or if, say, you feel depressed. All you're required to do is to look inward and trust what you see—or don't see! You'll find several experiments at the end of this book. Let me emphasize the importance of *doing* these experiments. *Reading* about your True Nature without *experiencing* It is as pointless and frustrating as browsing through travel brochures but never going on holiday. And since the View pointed out by the experiments is right where you are and is free, there's no excuse for not looking! Be adventurous! Spend a few minutes doing the experiments. There's nothing to lose and everything to gain.

Once you've seen Who you really are, simply go on seeing, attending to, and drawing on this Resource each and every day. This never-ending practice is endlessly nourishing. Though it may not always give you what you want, it gives you what you really need. Be conscious of the Truth, and the Truth will not only free you, but will care for you, as well.

Now in his nineties, Douglas Harding grew up among the Exclusive Plymouth Brethren in Suffolk, England. Having rejected their narrow fundamentalism when he was 21, Harding began questioning society's assumptions about what it is to be human. After ten years of sustained inquiry, he stumbled upon the glaringly obvious presence of the Source—in the very center and heart of himself. (Our True Nature is well-hidden by being so obvious!) Suddenly, Harding was *seeing* the Source, not merely imagining or thinking about it.

The result of this awakening was a truly great work of philosophy, *The Hierarchy of Heaven and Earth: A New Diagram of Man in the Universe*, published in condensed form in 1952 and described by C.S. Lewis as "a work of the highest genius." Superbly written and drawing deeply on all the sciences, the arts, and religion, it is a fresh, contemporary view of our place in the universe – or of the universe's place in us. It reveals that each of us is a vital and wholly meaningful part of the Whole—indeed, that each *is* the Whole. As well as being true, this Self-portrait is breathtakingly beautiful and, in spite of all the evil in the world finds love to be of the essence. In 1961 Harding published his next book, *On Having No Head*, a short spiritual classic containing a dramatic description of his awakening to his True Nature (See page xv). Since then he has written many more books.

I met Douglas Harding in 1970 and almost immediately found myself committed to both practicing and sharing this Way. Recently I reread almost all of Harding's writings, looking for quotations for this book. It was an inspiring experience. I have also taken quotations from audio and video tapes of interviews and lectures. Obviously, the words in this selection spoke to me; someone else would make different choices. I believe, however, that this selection faithfully represents Harding and his message. It gives a good view of him as a teacher, philosopher, writer, and spiritual friend. It shows his broad and deep application of *The Headless Way* to daily life—how well it works out in practice— including his comments on relationships, creativity, love, stress, coping with problems, and death.

What also comes through is Harding's irrepressible curiosity about life; his delight and joy; his humor, energy and humanity; as well as the originality, clarity, and poetry of his writing. Woven through all this is Harding's deep conviction in the practicality of trusting Who you really are—surrendering to the will of God—and his infectious astonishment at the "impossible" miracle of Being. As he says, "There really shouldn't be anything at all!" Yet, astoundingly, there is: Being—Self-inventing itself and this extraordinary universe, all in full working order! How on earth does It do it?

Douglas Harding is a man who "by happy chance," much hard work, and the grace of God has found his way home from his temporary appearance to his eternal Reality, completing this journey not as a person, of course, but as Reality itself (the only way to do it). He continues making this journey each day back to the place one never leaves. He has helped many others travel this same path—the "one meter path," as he calls it—and during more than forty years of giving talks and workshops all over the world has made many friends. He has given a great gift to the world – an open Way home to the Open Source from which all things freely and eternally flow. May his words inspire you to travel home to the place you never left and to enjoy each day being open to the Source.

—Richard Lang
London, England

TOTAL ABSENCE

From On Having No head

The best day of my life—my rebirthday, so to speak—was when I found I had no head. This is not a literary gambit, a witticism designed to arouse interest at any cost. I mean it in all seriousness: *I have no head*.

It was eighteen years ago, when I was thirty-three, that I made the discovery. Though it certainly came out of the blue, it did so in response to an urgent enquiry; I had for several months been absorbed in the question *What am I?* The fact that I happened to be walking in the Himalayas at the time probably had little to do with it, though in that country unusual states of mind are said to come more easily. However that may be, a very still clear day, and a view from the ridge where I stood—over misty blue valleys to the highest mountain range in the world—made a setting worthy of the grandest vision.

What actually happened was something absurdly simple and unspectacular: I stopped thinking. A peculiar quiet, an odd kind of alert limpness or numbness, came over me. Reason and imagination and all mental chatter died down. For once, words really failed me. Past and future dropped away. I forgot who and what I was—my name, manhood, animalhood, all that could be called mine. It was as if I had been born that instant, brand new, mindless, innocent of all memories. There existed only the Now, that present moment and what was clearly given in it. To look was enough. And what I found was khaki trouser legs terminating downwards in a pair of brown shoes, khaki sleeves terminating sideways in a pair of pink hands, and a khaki shirtfront terminating upwards in . . . absolutely nothing whatever! Certainly not in a head.

It took me no time at all to notice that this nothing, this hole where a head should have been, was no ordinary vacancy, no mere nothing. On the contrary, it was very much occupied. It was a vast emptiness vastly filled, a nothing that found room for everything—room for grass, trees, shadowy distant hills, and far above them snow peaks like a row of angular clouds riding the blue sky. I had lost a head and gained a world.

It was all quite literally breathtaking. I seemed to stop breathing altogether, absorbed in the Given. Here it was, this superb scene brightly shining in the clear air, alone and unsupported, mysteriously suspended in the void, and (*and* this was the real miracle, the wonder and delight) utterly free of "me," unstained by any observer. Its total presence was my total absence, body and soul.

Lighter than air, clearer than glass, altogether released from myself, I was nowhere around. Yet in spite of the magical and uncanny quality of this vision, it was no dream, no esoteric revelation. Quite the reverse: it felt like a sudden waking from the sleep of ordinary life, an end to dreaming. It was self-luminous reality, for once swept clean of all obscuring mind. It was the revelation, at long last, of the perfectly obvious. It was a lucid moment in a confused life history. It was a ceasing to ignore something that (since early childhood, at any rate) I had always been too busy or too clever to see. It was naked, uncritical attention to what had all along been staring me in the face—my utter facelessness. In short, it was all perfectly simple and plain and straightforward, beyond argument, thought, and words. There arose no questions, no reference beyond the experience itself, but only peace and a quiet joy, and the sensation of having dropped an intolerable burden.

REALITY

*It all boils down to
this simple thing:*

What am I in my own
experience at this
time? What am I
looking out of—
because that's real,
that's my reality, as
distinct from my
appearance for you.

APPEARANCE

When we join the human club we become
eccentric by about a meter and we lose
touch with our Source; we lose the
meaning of our lives.
We are in deep, deep trouble.

It can all be summed up in a few words:
I am what I look like.

Well, I'm not. I'm the *opposite* of what I look like.

You've got what I look like, it's your problem
and you're welcome to it. I'm looking after where
it's *coming from*, which is this Awake Mystery,
Space, Capacity, Stillness, Immensity,
visibly in receipt of the world.

ONE

I am at large in the world. I can discover no
watcher here, and over there something watched,
no peep-hole out into the world, no windowpane,
no frontier. I do not detect a universe:
it lies wide open to me.

*Spiritual things are truly physical, and truly physical
things are spiritual. There is no division.*

*This center is the spaceless bud that is never and yet
always bursting into the immense flower of my
many-regioned space.*

Don't imagine that turning *in* to this imperishable
No-thing is turning *away* from that world of
perishing things, ceasing to be with it,
involved, caring.

When I overlook the Space I accord them here, I miss-see them. But when I look "only" at this Space, I get them thrown in for a bonus because the Space is always and absolutely united with its contents. Looking out, I get barely half the story; looking in, I get it all.

Whether I advertise it or not, this organization that I am has a vacancy for a universe.

GOD

God is indivisible.

This is so marvelous because it means the whole of
God is where you are—not your little bit of God,
but the whole of God.

If we resist this, it's because we are resisting our
splendor, our greatness. The wonderful proposition
of all the mystics that I know and would care to
call real mystics is that the heart of you, the reality
of your life, the reality of your being, your real self
is the whole of God—not a little bit of that fire,
but the *whole* fire.

To lack divinity is to lack being.

BEING

The wisdom of
humanity, of our
species, is at your very
center, nearer to you than all
else. Where you come from,
what you look out of, is not a
product of the world but the
Origin of the world,
the Mystery.

Call it what you like:
Atman-Brahman,
Buddha-Nature, Allah,
God, Indwelling Christ—
it has many names.

This is more "me,"
more central to me,
than how I am perceived.

What I operate from,
what I live out of,
what I live from,
is Being itself. Being!

NONDUALITY

I find it makes no sense to write off one of these
two—either the Center or the Periphery—as *real*
and the other as *unreal*, or else as somewhat less
real and fundamental, less truly ME,
than the other.

I find it makes little sense, either, to say that one of
them *depends* on the other. That my nonphysical
consciousness here has that physical world for its
basis. Or, vice versa, that that world is an
accident—a casual and unnecessary sport or
projection—of this Consciousness that lies
here at the heart of it. They are of a piece,
presented together, and not served up separately.
I don't so much understand or
believe this as see it.

For instance, I SEE, right now, that this Emptiness
here *is*—rather than contains—these shapes and
these colors, this page and these hands.

As Zen insists, form is void and void is form;
Nirvana is none other than *Samsara*; the Lotus of
Enlightenment is one with the Swamp of Delusion
that is its habitat. Whenever I exalt one of the
pair at the expense of the other, I'm in trouble,
and my enemy Death has got hold of me. God is as
null without his world as it is null without him.

But when I perceive—when I consciously live—
their absolute unity, I embrace Death as my friend.
Even for God—especially for God—
there is, as the saying goes,
always something.

11

Consciousness isn't a thing to be split up and shared among things. It is the unique prerogative, the boundless Essence of the First Person singular, present tense.

What I experience depends upon many things: the state of my physical and chemical layers, my brain, my body, my world, and ultimately the whole of things.

That I experience depends upon No-thing. Awareness is the function of—it *is*—this unbounded Emptiness at the heart of my many-layered world.

To imagine it lurking
in third persons as such
is as common as it is
absurd, and as absurd
as it is distressing.

It's not as if, arriving at this No-man's-land and No-thing's-land—or, if you like, this Never-never-land—one comes to a *dead* end, to a region so nonexistent that it could hold no meaning and excite no interest.

Exactly the reverse.

It is that Unknowable from whose depths the known gushes without reason and without stint, that Unthinkable Seed of all life and all thought—including *this* thought about it.

14

UNKNOWABLE

Search as I may, I can find no decision making or maker, no ideas or feelings or impressions of my own— bright or dull—no mind at all but only this bare Consciousness or Awakeness that reads as absolutely clueless, useless, incompetent, idiotic. Yet, what's needed is coming up from the depths just when it should. In Heaven you discover this quiet upsurge from the Abyss.

Try it out, learn to trust it, and go on relying on it more and more. Here is never-failing inspiration for nonpersons.

CREATIVITY

*In ordinary life we find hints of the vital
connection between Self-awareness and creativity.*

Don't our very best moments always include a
heightened consciousness of ourselves, so that we
aren't really lost in inspiration or creative
fervor or love, but newly found?

At its finest, doesn't the opaque object over
there point unmistakably back to
the transparent Subject here?

It may even happen that the transparency
comes first: we attend, our idiotic chatter
dies down, we consciously become
nothing but this alert, expectant Void—
and presently the required tune or picture,
the key notion, the true answer, arises
ready-made in that Void,
from that Void.

*If we wish to find out what it's really like to
create the world, we have only to desire
nothing and pay attention.*

PROBLEMS

The true function of problems is to direct
you to their solution at the Center.

Having some problems is very helpful.

Having quite severe problems brings me
back to the place where there are no problems.
Because Who I really, really am is problem-free.
I'm living from the problem-free area
out into the world.

Part of the price of involvement in the world is
to have feelings, some of which are agreeable,
some of which are disagreeable,
some of which are tragic.

I can't exist, can't express at all
without this dualism:
the dualism of good and evil, beauty and
ugliness, black and white, etc., which is the
inescapable condition of expressing into
the world from the place that is
free of those dualities.

PROBLEM - FREE

At the center of my life
is this Awareness whose
very nature I find is
freedom—freedom not
only from thinghood,
but from thoughts and
feelings of all kinds.

Certainly free from
problems of all kinds. As
the source of those things,
the origin of those
difficult things, its
business must be to leave
them alone, free to be what
they are.

Who I really am doesn't in itself change what I like to call my human nature. What it does is to place it. This difficult and sometimes heartrending stuff is not denied. In fact, it is far more honestly reckoned with and cheerfully taken on board, from the state of freedom at the center, than ever it was from that illusory person.

It's not a case of being free from these things in the sense that one abolishes them, but of being free from them in the sense that one locates them. They are no longer central. This awareness not only removes one from them—without removing oneself from them—but in the long run and when persisted in, it changes them.

SHIFT

This seeing is believing.

Altogether unmystical (in the popular sense), it is a precise, total, all-or-nothing experience admitting of no degrees. Relief is instant and complete—so long as it lasts. But now the really exacting part of the work begins: You have to go on seeing your Absence/Presence whenever and wherever you can, until the seeing becomes quite natural (repeat *natural*) and unbroken. This is neither to lose yourself in your Emptiness nor in what fills it, but *simultaneously* to view the thing you are looking at and the No-thing you are looking out of.

There will be found no times when this two-way attention is out of place.

The price of sanity is vigilance.

What's the good of *talking about*
this world-transforming shift of
viewpoint without *making* the
shift, and going on to stay shifted?

How to do just that?

Cultivate the habit of *seeing* that
in fact it's no shift at all, but
simply being where you were all
along, at the world's Center.

NO-MIND

Basically, the trouble with my mind is the conviction I've got one, and returning it to the Universe at large is enough to set it in order.

It's really very inefficient to operate from a mind that is full of things to go wrong, and so efficient to operate from a No-mind that is empty of all that chatter. This isn't a dogma for believing, but a working hypothesis for testing, all day and every day. It's never too late to have a marvelous childhood. True maturity is that second childhood that I call alert idiocy.

One's mind awakens. Ideas, inspiration, guidance from moment to moment, flow without obstruction from their Source, which is experienced here as Itself mindless.

I am truly broad-minded to the degree that
my mind, let go of, alights on and merges
with and irradiates the whole scene.
There it comes into its own.

To be opinionated, narrow-minded, under
pressure, depressed, repressed—all such
diseases of the mind arise from its
displacement and resulting compression.
Given back to the world, returned to where
it came from, it expands and recovers.

At large again, it is
infinitely vast and
generous.

What is the heart

and substance of love?

We are built for loving. We are built to die for each other, to disappear in each other's favor.

> Until the loss of one's head issues in the finding of one's heart—a heart so tender that it is mortally wounded by the world's appalling suffering— one falls far short of the goal, which is the love that transmutes all suffering.

Truly it is one of the unforeseen pleasures of the First Person life to gaze unabashed into the faces of one's friends, without feeling or thinking anything in particular, and just see them for what they always were—*things for looking at and never for looking out of.*

This isn't an unloving state, reducing you
to a cardboard cutout. Quite the reverse.

It is a most loving refusal
to separate my
Consciousness from
yours, and it removes
the last barrier
between us.
Liberated from the
superstition of plural
spirits, we are at last really
one.

This is the perfect love that casts out fear.

LOVE

B E L I E F

The steady assumption of every grown-up, the basis of his life as a man among men (all the more massive for remaining unexamined) is that there lies at the center of his universe a solid, opaque, colored, complicated, active *thing*, mostly invisible to its owner but nevertheless perfectly real.

This universal human conviction isn't spelled out in so many words. It doesn't need to be; it's too evident, it goes without saying.

And it's a lie! Actually, it's the lie.

The gigantic superstructure of our life is falling apart because so much of it is built on quicksand—on unexamined quicksand, at that.

In plain language, it's the basic assumptions that you and I make about ourselves and our status in the world—and hence about the world itself—that are the trouble.

Whatever I'm doing from the delusion and nonsense that there is a thing here doing it is worse done.

Whatever I'm doing from my Space is better done.

LIVING FROM TRUTH

There's no occasion in our working or
leisure life when it's inappropriate or
inefficient to live from the truth. The
truth, so easy to see, is so hard to keep on
seeing. But is life without it less hard? Is
life lived from a many-sided lie a
practical proposition?

It's never practical or healthy to live
from a lie of any sort, but when that lie
is about one's essential Nature—
look out!
Or rather, look in!

Attend, as if for the first time, to the one
Spot in the world that only you are in a
position to inspect, to the Point that only
you have inside information about, and
witness its immediate explosion to
worldwide dimensions.

LIVING
FROM SPACE

Do what you like to me, I will
live from what I *see* is here, not
from what you *say* is here. I will
tell the world about it, and I will
take the consequences.
Meanwhile, I swear to you
that to live from *this* is
really to live, which is
to live Godly.

The primary and saving whole
truth is that we are all living from
our Space and not our face, all
doing it right, all firmly and
forever established in our
True Nature.

To be at all is to be Being.

In this sense all are awakened.

In the last resort there's

no other experience

than this Experience.

Only our Void

Nature is aware.

ENERGY

So thoroughly have we
insulated the human
from the cosmic that
when at last they are
brought together the
effect may well prove
overwhelming, as the
pent-up energy is
discharged in a flash of
illumination revealing
undreamed-of beauty.

Seeing Who I am is a strangely

physical experience.

It is like an energy; it is like an empowering,
a physical tone, an uplift, a rootedness,
courage, a faring forth into the world.
It is enlivening.

OUTCOME

The initial seeing into your Nature is simplicity
itself: once noticed, Nothing is so obvious! But it
is operative only in so far as it is practiced. The
results—freedom from greed and hate and fear
and delusion—are assured only while the
One they belong to isn't overlooked.

Absence is for acceptance as absence,
not as the presence of a well-concealed
gold mine. The gold comes out all right,
but unsought, in its own good time
and unpredictable shape.

It would be difficult to overstate the
practical importance of this discovery, its
consequences for everyday living.

All alienation, all separation, the many-sided
threat of hostile things and persons and
situations—these are no more than bad dreams.

Be patient.
Don't demand
that these or any
other blessings be
apparent at once.

YES!

I don't mean gritting your teeth and putting on a
ghastly smile and saying YES! to all that's
happening to you, regardless, as a duty and
a discipline.

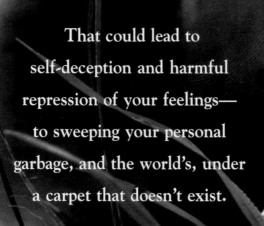

That could lead to
self-deception and harmful
repression of your feelings—
to sweeping your personal
garbage, and the world's, under
a carpet that doesn't exist.

No:

See things for what they are, exactly as
given in your Emptiness—in this
Openness which manifestly has no
preferences, no resistances or
resentments, no checklist of good and
bad things, no categories of beautiful
and ugly, acceptable and unacceptable.

*And see what comes from paying attention
to the way you already are.*

See how perfectly you are built for this
job of willing what is. See how proper
and natural it is for you. And just allow
(don't force) the joy to arise, the peace
that comes from having nothing to
complain about. Given half a chance, it
surely will, perhaps much sooner than
you imagine possible.

MIND AT LARGE

My mind, with all its thoughts and feelings, is
centrifugal. Ceasing to be a small, local,
private, personal possession abstracted from
the universe there, and shut up in a brain-box
here (as if it could be!), my mind is at large,
one with the universe, blown sky-high.

The world, so seen, is the same old world,
yet utterly different.

It is replete with a mind and meaning I
no longer abstract from it. It is *all there,*
because I claim none of it for myself.
It is sane. It makes sense. It is loved.

I'm free at last to enjoy people and the world just as they come, from this their Empty Source.

A W A K E

What is Awakening, Enlightenment, Realization?
Awakening from what? Enlightenment as to what?
Realization of what?

It is waking up from all your dreams and
imaginings and preconceptions, becoming
enlightened as to the given facts, realizing what
you clearly are in your first-hand experience right
now. It is being perfectly honest to yourself about
yourself, at last. It is having the courage and
effrontery, even the idiocy, to go by what you see,
instead of by what you are told. It is questioning
all mental habits and conventional assumptions,
however commonsensible or sanctified. It is total
open-mindedness, transparency, simplicity and
taking nothing for granted.

In one word, it is *discovery*.

What is to be discovered is your own nature.
Who are you? Only you are in a position to find
out because everyone else is elsewhere, off-center.
Only you can investigate what it is to be you.

There exists for none of us, not even for the most
"spiritual," a merely human or personal liberation
that leaves out the natural world. There's no such
thing as a true enlightenment that doesn't light up
every creature on Earth and in the skies, however
grotesque or remote or unlovable. How could we
begin to disentangle ourselves from any part of the
One in whom we live and move and have our
being?

**Enlightenment is cosmic
or an illusion.**

UNMOVED
MOVER

The art of handling these
inexorable goings-on is
the art of resting on what
underlies them . . .

. . . *the art and*
science of consciously being the
ground that supports all that
commotion without itself becoming
disturbed in the slightest.

Here, you are the bedrock of the world, where it all begins and where it all ends. Eternally one and the same, you are the Unmoved Mover.

The great obstacle is self-satisfaction, absence of need. How much that man loses who, because he is so good at being human, is never driven to find out what else he is! He cannot gain even this world if he loses his soul, which belongs to all the worlds.

It is the worst kind of eccentricity to be so well-balanced that you are never upset in the direction of the Whole.

HELPING
THE WORLD

When you see the truth, you are
doing it for others as much as for
yourself because Who is doing it is
not an individual. Who is doing it is
the One who is the inside story of
all these contestants on the face of
the Earth.

Our enlightenment cannot help but spill out on all
beings, for the simple reason that we *are* them.

If I'm suffering from this disease of
confrontation in my relationship with you at
this moment, what's the use of trying to deal
with the same problem of confrontation at
other levels—national and international—
confrontation between sexes, ethnic groups,
religions, ideologies, power blocs, and so on?
In other words, service to the world begins at
home because when you've found out Who
you are, you find you are the world.

When I identify with the guy in the mirror,
he turns his back on the world. He says, "I've
got enough troubles of my own. Keep out."
The One you really are never can turn her
back on the world. She embraces the world.
She *is* the world. This is not because you are
special; you were always this way.

Exactly what (I ask myself) is this shocking
He, this shameless She, this unbowdlerized
It, in reality?
Its essence is Awareness, the One Light of
Consciousness that lights up the world and every
creature the world comes into. I locate this Light
Indivisible right where I am, plumb in the Center
of this world as I find it, nearer than near,
at the heart of the heart of me.

> *Here is no spark of that Fire,*
> *but the blazing Furnace itself.*

Look around you for a million years, ransack the
universe, probe with every instrument into
everything, and nowhere and nowhen will you find
a glimmer of consciousness, a will that is not your
will, a hint of a hint of another I AM.

Never will you find anything or anyone faintly
resembling this Self-being of yours: It is absolutely
unique, one-time, and indescribable.

All of God is right where you are now
and nowhere else. I AM is one. There
is no second I AM to stand in
your light, to put up
the feeblest opposition.

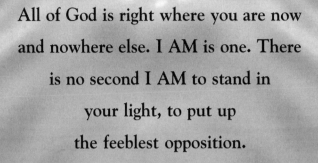

HEART CENTER

All is as you
would have it
because you are
Who you are.

GLORY

Don't believe but test what I'm saying to
you: that all things, never mind what, when
consciously observed from their Origin,
are bathed in its perfume and lit
up with its
radiance.

There is a glory. Always.
To find it, be Where it comes from.

No way can you shrug off your mystery and your
grandeur. No way can you get out of being— at
the end of the day that has no beginning or end—
the Best and the Greatest,
the One and Only.

How much harder
   it is to bear one's splendor
     than one's miseries!

THE ALONE

To realize one's true nature is to realize that one is the only One that is.

This is a paradoxical combination of worship, admiration, and wonder for the One, while at the same time realizing that all this is the experience of the One by the One.

One's own Self-awareness is none other than God's own Self-awareness.

The only real remedy for your loneliness is your Aloneness. And this Aloneness is the crown of all experience, the brightest gem in that crown.

There is only one, the Alone, and there is only
one place where one will find the Alone:

Never in others, never
out there, but only
in *here*, where
consciousness is given.

Consciousness is only
given in one place—all
of it is given here,
and all of it is
given now.

REAL

This Void is not mere emptiness; it is not mere absence; it is Self-aware.

It is Self-awareness itself, and that makes it quite different from a void that is just an unconscious absence. Secondly, it is full to overflowing, full of what it's entertaining. Thirdly, it says to itself, "This is for real. I am this. I AM." It has its own interior self-justification.

It is self-validating from within and, when experienced, cannot be doubted. It is, after all, what I'm most sure of because I am it. All else is mere hearsay, off-center, remote, changing, inscrutable, a product of ignorance. This Clarity I know because I am it. Here I have inside information, and only here. All the rest is external acquaintance.

For all these good reasons I say it is real and all else is comparatively unreal.

One seeks in vain for labels, worthy labels that will stick to this Nonexistence, which is infinitely more real than any of its products, than anything that exists.

POWER

As Divinity itself, as the Space for all and the
Source of all, you are responsible for all. There is
no second Power. Who you really, really are did it
all, is doing it all. But notice whether this Space
that you are is *efforting* its contents. Do you, who
are attending to the scene, have any sense of
intending it, of contriving it and cobbling it
together, of causing and maintaining it? It is for
you, who are responsible for it, to say.

Isn't it rather that everything flows
spontaneously, without motive or taking thought,
from your Being, a ceaseless spin-off from
Who you are?

The list of the things that even you can't do is endless.

All the same, you are
all-powerful in the
sense that, accepting
the coexistence and
clash of opposites as the
price (a terribly high
price, but not prohibitive)
of a cosmos, you let out an
almighty YES! to it all—
YES throughout it all and
in spite of it all, YES
because this (in all its
astounding and awful and
lovely detail) is what you
are, and YES because
you *will* what you are.

YOU

When you start living the heroic life—that is,
living from your true Nature—your
peripheral and human nature
is bound to benefit.

All is You.

You cannot know in advance how or when, but you can count on Yourself, the superhuman hero, to give yourself, the human nonhero, a helping hand and a leg up where necessary.

How could you fear Yourself?
How could you despise, resent,
be bored by Yourself?

How could you
not love Yourself?

SELF-ORIGINATION

Does the
miraculous (no, impossible!)
uprush of the Self-originating One from
primordial chaos and darkest night, without help or
reason—hoisting Himself into existence by his own
nonexistent bootstraps—astound and delight you?

If so, I can assure you that it is you as Him, and
certainly not you as Jane or Henry or whoever,
who are amazed, who are filled with admiration,
who jump for joy into the very special Joy
that's born of that very special and
never-ceasing Miracle.

The Miracle of His Self-creation, after which the
creation of billions of universes, all going
strong, is nothing special, a
matter of routine.

In the Kingdom of Heaven, you are much more efficient.

Here, you come to recognize and increasingly give way to the practical flair, the astounding know-how, of the very Source of things. More and more, Who you are is allowed to look after what you are, unhindered. The technique is very simple and very precise—and by no means automatic. It is this: whatever you are attending to there, you attend also to the Attender here, so that your gaze is at least as much inward as outward. You see yourself as Space for that—for those busy hands or feet doing their thing, for that strangely dexterous scalpel or brush or bow or chisel or pen, animated by the real Virtuoso.

In fewer and fewer circumstances do you overlook the Looker-Adept, until eventually it's impossible to do so. And gradually it sinks in that this is the very One who has the ultimate know-how, the "impossible" knack of being its own Origin and Inventor, of seeing to its own ceaseless emerging, for no reason and with no help.

KNOW-HOW

Consciously handing over to this Expert (not surprisingly) ensures that whatever is done, from the humblest of chores to the sublimest work of art, is better done—more smoothly and swiftly and pleasurably than it would be if a mere person had the sense of doing it.

Test it and see.

HUMILITY

Now, you may say that what we're talking about is blasphemous, that it is pride to find that where you are is none other than the mystery and majesty behind the universe.

The real pride is when I say I run a separate little corner shop of Being Here, in addition to and independent of, or quasi-independent of God, who runs a hypermarket of Being. Real humility says that my being is that Being.

Real humility is to see in what and in whom lies my being.

At the same time, this Reality is in a certain sense wholly other than me. That is to say, it is wholly mysterious and adorable and unknowable and extraordinary, the great Self-originating One from which all comes.

Here we sink our differences—or
rather, *we* sink and leave our
            differences floating. All
            action is stooping to
            conquer, where stooping
is absolute abasement.

Whereas the Experience of our Nature is served
up (if at all) complete, in one infinitely generous
helping, its meaning is for the most part
withheld. Normally it's doled out in driblets, at
other times poured out more generously,
but never given in its entirety.
The last word about This is never said,
the ultimate and all-embracing idea of it is never
conceived, the deepest feeling
never plumbed.

MEANING

Truly speaking, our Source has no meaning
whatever. In Itself It is infinitely beyond all
that limited and limiting stuff, for
nothing that can be said or
thought or felt about
It is It.

The Source of all meaning is Itself far
beyond and absolutely free from
all that proceeds from It.
And You are That.

FREEDOM

Freedom is free.

When I am consciously at large—no longer a
thing among things, a consciousness among
consciousnesses—I am Liberated, and
the world, in spite of everything,
is all right because it is all me.

Described negatively,
it's my way out of the tightest spot, my
escape route from the most secure of prisons.

Described positively,
it's my way in to the absolute
Liberty that I am.

PURPOSE

What is the purpose of life?
As I see it, and as the great mystics of all the great
religions saw it, the purpose of life is a simple
one: conscious union with our Source.

As Meister Eckhart said, "God's in, I'm out."
He said, "Put on your jumping shoes
and jump into God."

Jump from your appearance to your Reality.
It is our business to jump into the place
we never left.

HEALING

In plain language, my
psychological problems all
boil down to the problem of
my Identity.

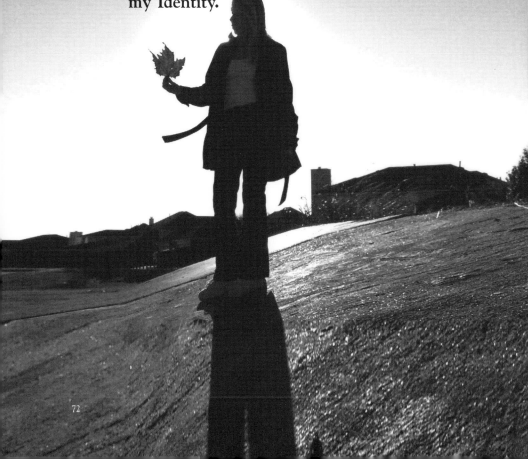

They are settled only by attending to the One here, to this First Person who is supposed to have them. Here is the only profound analysis, the only therapy that penetrates to the Root of the trouble, the only lasting cure of my disease. Though the results may be slow to manifest (and then be more manifest to others than to me), this way is economical, thorough, foolproof, well-tested over thousands of years, instantly available, and (though in a sense it costs the Earth) quite *gratis*.

We are all more or less ill until we find by Self-inquiry our Oneness with everyone else.

Only God, our Whole, is the completion, the healing remedy, of the fragments that we are. He is what we want, and we are not ourselves without Him. We are lost until we are lost in Him.

BOTTOM LINE

Above your Bottom Line is the
place of No-choice.

Everything there is caught
in a close-knit web of mutual
conditioning, and freedom is a dream.
The Bottom Line itself is the place of
Choice. Here is the only place where
freedom is real, seeing that there's nothing
to bind or be bound.

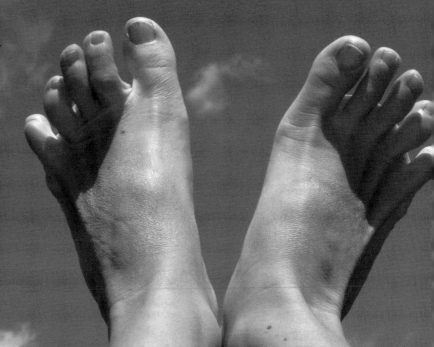

Our freedom does not consist in denying all that determines us and asserting our own self-will. On the contrary, its true ground is our willingness to accept every necessity, so that it ceases to be merely external.

We are free insofar as we join our will to God's.

We have the choice of His freedom or our bondage.

No longer so damned cocksure I know what it's like being me, I dare to start all over again and *bow before the evidence*—actually as well as metaphorically.

I bend and bow so deeply that I come to the very edge of me and my world, to the *Bottom Line* it all arises from—a frontier that doesn't prevent me from gazing past it and into the Infinite Source of All, brilliantly on display yet awesomely mysterious.

Here is not a case of *I am this or that or the other*, but plain I AM—and, back of the I AM, the I AM NOT from which it arises without reason and without stint.

MYSTERY

The bottom line is that I know myself as unknowable.

I'm rooted and grounded in complete mystery,

unknowability, ineffability, unawareness.

Here, completing my submission to the evidence, I
come to the most overlooked and underrated spot
in the world, the place that's replaced with
No-place, the Terminus of termini, unique,
baffling, the Mystery that's more than
worthy of my humblest
obeisance.

REDISCOVERY

The
discovery
that I am absolutely
all right as I am—as I AM—
has to be actualized by its patient
rediscovery, and rediscovery, and
rediscovery, until all traces of artifice
and effort, all sense of attainment, have
vanished.

*Until it has become in
ordinary day-to-day living
what it always was in
fact: one's natural
state.*

To un-thing yourself when all's going well is good
habit-forming practice. But un-thinging yourself
when all's going badly is better still. Then the act
of homing-in makes a deeper impression, and life
in the future is that much less likely to
catch you out, or napping.

While it's the easiest thing imaginable to see
yourself intermittently as bare Capacity, it's far
from easy to keep up the seeing.
What challenge can compare with this one great
adventure that is never completed, yet is ever
complete because you can enjoy being at the goal
from the very first step along the road?

WHOLENESS

This immense and self-aware
emptiness that I find here
isn't just empty.

It's empty-for-filling.

Ultimately, no one and nothing is left
      out. In fact I'm not well . . .
          not quite sane, not "all
          there," not whole
        until I'm
         the Whole.

To put it another way:
Is the universe whole while I split
it into an observer here and an
observed there, into a me-part
and a not-me part?

To enjoy the universe as a *Universe*,
and no longer to suffer from it as a
*Duo*verse, I have to be none of it
centrally, and all of it peripherally.

They are two sides
of the coin.

The basic doctrine of the Perennial Philosophy is
that you and I are God herself traveling
incognito. The one we all really are is the one
reality behind all things—call it God, Buddha-
nature, *Atman-Brahman*, what you like.

What one is doing is only to connect up with
and celebrate and live from this perennial
wisdom, which is to be found at the very heart of
all the great religions. There it is—
unrecognized, neglected, scorned,
denied—but there it is.

At the very core of the great religious traditions—
overlaid, neglected, very often vehemently
denied by religious experts, but nevertheless the
taproot those traditions spring from and are
sustained by—is one perfectly lucid,
simple, awesome, beautiful realization.
It's a proclamation about *you*.

PERENNIAL
PHILOSOPHY

No mere spark are you of that
Eternal Fire, no mere ray of the One
Light that lights every man and woman
and child that the world comes into.

You are all of that All,
which is strictly indivisible.

TRUE
SPIRITUALITY

Until I locate for certain my humanness in its
proper place out there among all those other
humans, until I hold it out there in my bare hands,
there is always the danger that it will succeed in
creeping here and infecting my Divine Center,
and will go on to reduce it to a horrendous—
indeed devilish—delusion of
grandeur.

What I find difficult and unacceptable really, is the
wishy-washy reliance on words, on concepts, of so
much alleged spirituality. True spirituality is real,
down to earth, concrete—it's coming home
from your appearance to your reality.

As the Buddha said, you won't by going reach that
place where there is the end of suffering.
You'll get it by coming.
We are so good at looking *that* way,
and lousy at looking *this* way.

Nirvana is the shore that's washed by the ocean
of *Samsara*, their meeting place; and Wisdom is
the contemplation of that shore as absolutely
bare and empty. Relief from suffering is found
by basing oneself on, by consciously coming
from that ineffable but conspicuous shoreline.

GRATEFUL

It's not a miracle that is
happening somewhere else.
It's taking place right Here,
right Here.

You are a magician bringing
yourself out of this hat of
Non-Being, and you haven't a
clue how you are doing it.

*I take my stand on that which I
cannot understand.*

I am grateful
for the miracle of Being.

In the last resort, one is grateful and astounded
that there isn't just nothing, a dark
night of nonexistence.

KNOWLEDGE

I don't know what I think until I
hear what I say—hear the
words that come from
my No-mouth.

It takes a lifetime of study to persuade us that we know nothing to speak of.

The mystics confirm and round off this conclusion, asserting that perfect knowledge of the object of highest rank is knowing that it is perfectly incomprehensible.

The first work of explanation is to render the mysterious commonplace; but it goes on to render the commonplace mysterious; and its work is unfinished so long as we feel that we know anything whatsoever.

*Only in knowing our total ignorance
do we overcome it.*

Are we face-to-face, in symmetrical relationship,
object confronting object, each shutting out the
other? Quite the contrary. Here where I am is no
face, no speck of anything to ward you off with, to
resist your invasion. Whether I like it or not, I'm
so wide open to you that your face is mine and I
have no other.

INTIMACY

This is an intimacy that is the paradigm
of all intimacy, infinitely deep and total,
immensely satisfying—once I have the
humility and the courage to notice it.
The awareness is crucial. I am fully
conscious of the perfect way you give me
your face, of the perfect way I take it.

The practical difference this discovery
makes to your relationships is immense
and cumulative. In fact, what it comes to
is that you aren't *related* in any way to
anyone: you *are* that one.

SCIENCE

The spirituality that denies
the universally accepted
findings of modern science at
all levels, or refuses to face up
to them and cheerfully take
them on board, is a pathetic
and moribund travesty of
spirituality.

Conversely, the spirituality
that perceives in these
findings a rich and precious
and indeed divine revelation
of our time and for our time
and just what's needed to
treat our sorry condition,
is alive and kicking.

While allowing that our modern science is valid and indeed indispensable as far as it goes, I claim that the ancient wisdom goes much further, that it is in a real sense more scientific and more sensible than science, as we know it, could ever be, and is in fact its practical and theoretical complement.

In other words, I maintain that Western objective science is only half of real science (the other half being the science of the Subject or First Person) and that we are in trouble because we mistake it for the whole.

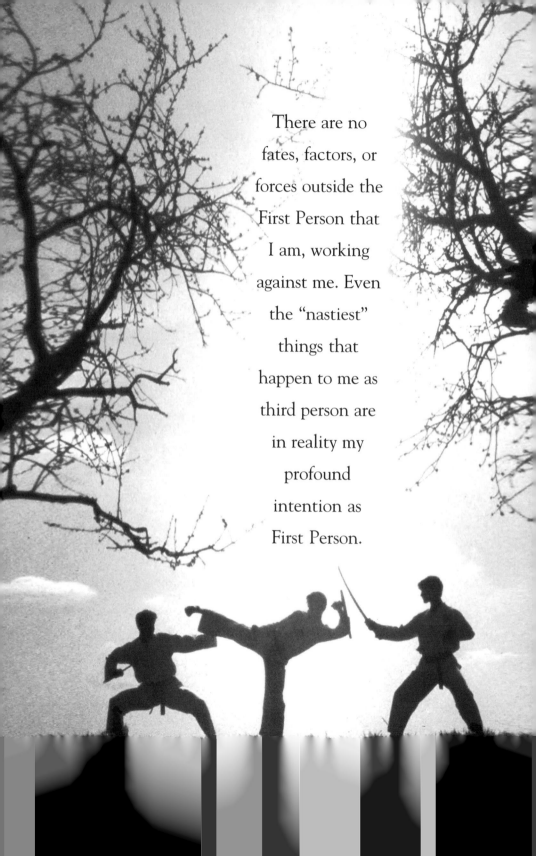

There are no fates, factors, or forces outside the First Person that I am, working against me. Even the "nastiest" things that happen to me as third person are in reality my profound intention as First Person.

FORCES

So I say YES! to life,

and this is the true therapy.

FEAR

It is always the *other* that I fear, hate, envy, plan to destroy. Prove to me that there's a level on which I *am* you and you *are* me—and all aspects of our mutual alienation are ended.

Here, I'm enjoying that face of yours as mine.
Here, I *have* you as object and *am* you as
subject, and so take on both your appearance
and your reality. What could be more intimate
than this double intimacy?

How could I fear you who are myself?

No wonder the essential Experience is
dismissed so cavalierly, is so unwelcome and so
distrusted: Below the surface, we are all
terrified of our Emptiness. Until its
inexhaustible and breathtaking beneficence
and fertility begin to take shape, it must seem
not just meaningless but suicidal,
mere annihilation.

Yet it's no bad thing to be fearful, provided
we're driven to the one refuge from all danger
and stress and fear – to this incomparable
Safety, to the Place or No-place we
have been all along.

LOSE ALL

My worldwide wheels can neither exist nor turn
without this unmoving hub; my worldwide body
has no organ half so vital as this subvital and
indeed subphysical heart of hearts. Here are key
and keyhole and door in one—the central
emptiness that is the key of the Kingdom, the
keyhole that leads to Wonderland, the needle's
eye that is the gate of Heaven.

GAIN ALL

Through this Point of entry I am in all the world
and all the world is in me. And if, having entered, I
am capable of many things, it is because capability
means room; if I am a thinking reed it is because,
reed-like, I am coreless. *Cogito ergo NON sum.* And
common sense, forever trying to salvage some
miserable chattel for me, only breaks the conditions
of that universal policy of insurance whereby
unlimited compensation is given to those
who lose all.

Your true Nature is the Paradox to take care of all
paradoxes: There is nothing that is not you and
nothing that is you; the Aware Space is and isn't its
contents; you care and you don't care; you control
things and they just happen.

PARADOX

This may sound silly, but in fact it is the
perfection of wisdom. And it works.

Spiritual life is all paradox. It's the union of
opposites. It's having your cherry cake
and eating it.

It finds you on the way Home and all the
way Home, seated, with your feet up,
by the fire of God's love.

The strange thing about suffering is that by taking
it on you go through to the underlying
peace that passes understanding.
Some people seem to suggest that when you see
Who you are, there is no more suffering.

On the contrary.
In a way, it's the exact
opposite of that.

You take it all on.

You take on the pain of creation,
not only human suffering but the whole
tragic history of the world and the suffering
of other creatures—not because you are a
saint or a good person. You have no
option. That's the way you are
made, and that's the way
through.

SUFFERING

I'm not saying, mind you, that a
life consciously lived from its true
Center will be safe or painless, easy
or consistently joyful.

Real adventure is made of sterner stuff. You
embrace the suffering of the world no less than
its splendor and its thrill.

The real joy, the joy that casts no
shadow and knows no
variation, has come
through the fire.

You could say that
the remedy for
suffering is
homeopathic.

The solution to a problem, no matter *what* it is, is
to see *whose* it is. Not to understand or feel or
think who has the problem, but actually to gaze on
that WHO and await what comes of the gazing.
This seeing and this waiting you can always do,
whatever your need.

The rest is out of your hands.

See, see what happens,
and trust it.

FAITH

Trust Who
you are to
come up
with the
right
answer
at the
right
time.

LOVING

If we really
look, surely
we can see
we are
built for
loving.

We are built
open,
as capacity for
the other
one.

If one experiences oneself as space for the other, one listens, one looks, one attends to the other. And the other one feels attended to, feels entertained and valued, because after all if you have nothing where you are, no face, no thing at all, that other one is doing you a marvelous service of supplying you with this fascinating scene.

It means that I am going to let others be what they are, because space has no way of manipulating and using and exploiting them. Space is very patient, very hospitable.

This is a totally different thing from the imagined basis of our personal relationships, which is a symmetrical one.

In a certain sense it is the very basis of loving.

UNITY

To every being, accordingly, I say—not lightly but
with all my heart: Here in the depths of me, as
Who I really, really am, I am the One
you really, really are.

Though we may belong to vastly different
regions and eras, wear vastly different faces,
enjoy vastly different experiences of the world,
all these are peripheral matters, matters of
accident and time and content,

They are transcended in the one central, timeless
Container and Essence in which I'm aware of
myself as you, and you, and you, ad infinitum.

**The barriers
are down, our
wounds are
healed, and we
are well again
because we are
One again.**

Rest assured that one moment of seeing
yourself as "Empty-for-all" affects
all profoundly.

Your best contribution to the future isn't
what you say, or even what you work for,
but what you *are* now. Nothing is so
catching as this well-founded
freedom from stress, this
impersonal serenity that
    must embrace all
        persons.

EVOLUTION

I very much believe that if there is to be a next big step in our evolution, it will be this step to our Center. The step from our present kind of consciousness will be to the new kind of First Person, concentric consciousness. Utopia would be in no danger of breaking out, but just imagine the Renaissance!

Seeing Who one is, is getting to the Center from which a light shines on the mind. One is under fewer illusions as to one's weaknesses, one's hangups, one's dubious motives and so on.

We have to go through the stage of discovering and being responsible for our unique selves.

But if that's the whole of the story, gosh I'm in deep trouble, because that little one—that face-thing in the mirror—is my certificate of loneliness, of meaninglessness, because a world consisting only of things is meaningless. Love has no place there. Freedom has no place. It's a world where each is celebrating its own separate individuality—a recipe for hell.

Hell says, "Keep out! I've got enough problems of my own."

RESPONSIBILITY

The First Person cannot turn his back on the
world. He faces the world. This is why we
resist our First Personhood. We have a feeling
that to see Who we really are is to take on the
suffering of the world—and the joy of the
world, what there is of it.

EXPECTATION

All things are

stressed.

By imagining yourself to be one of those things,
you *take on* its stresses. But seeing that in fact you
are empty for that thing, you *let go* of its stresses.
To deny what you are is to suffer stress.

To get to Heaven, let life floor you.

Life is guaranteed to do just that, to let you
down—all the way into the Safety Net
that will never let you down.

Expect *nothing* of the Nothing
that underscores life, and
it cannot disappoint.

Also expect *everything* of it,
and again it cannot
disappoint.

It's being so mock-modest in our demands on life,
expecting *something* of it—this or that particular
rose, and with no thorns attached—
which is the stress-maker, and prevents our
enjoyment of the rose garden.

Truly I forget in what my wealth and
true grandeur lie, how inexhaustible
they are, and how my title to them
is my absolute poverty.

Plunging headfirst into the sea of
nothingness, I find there
untold treasure.

This is a very good bargain: to trade in
one tiny thing in the universe, to
exchange this one mortal non-okay
thing for the whole darn lot—
for the whole world.
It's so profitable!

WEALTH

By coming to look at ourselves from outside, we
lost this treasure, we lost this wealth, and we spend
the rest of our lives—alas, many of us—trying to
get back a part of our lost heritage.

When we see who we really are, we don't crave
unnecessary objects that are put there simply
for us to get some symbol or token
of our lost treasure.

When the world is yours, why go
for a million dollars?
Chicken feed!
   Pathetic!

ALWAYS
AVAILABLE

Seeing Who one is, is the root.

In my experience, it is without quality. It's
naked, absolutely naked, and that is why it
is so valuable—why it is available whatever one's mood. One doesn't have to
psych oneself up. The leaning back, the
comfort and the excitement, and the sense
of mystery and wonder with which This is
connected for me—all these, however rich
and important, seem to me to be just a
little downstream from the Seeing. And
this is a good thing because the Seeing, the
Clarity, unites us all even if and when we
don't appreciate the comfort and mystery
and when all seems gray and dull.

AUTHORITY

You are the authority, you the reader, the hearer,
the workshopee: *you are the authority, and Douglas is
a mere pointer.* What he writes, what he says, what
he does, is simply to direct you to the source
of all authority, yourSelf.

I thrust you back on your own resources.

Everything I say is for testing, nothing I say is for
taking on trust. The only authority is Who you are,
not your human nature but Who you really, really,
really are. All that I am doing is pointing to this.

If you find anything that I say
inconsistent with this authority
which is built into you, which you
indeed are, for God's sake say
"To hell with it!"

HIDE-AND-SEEK

To push home your inquiry into my existence is to destroy it, for I am always elsewhere, like a rainbow or a mirage. If I take myself as I am to myself, I find presented these men, trees, clouds, stars; and I scatter them all as if in a giant centrifuge, leaving the center empty.

If, instead, I take myself as I am to others, I am a host of creatures of numberless shapes and sizes; and all of them, though they belong out there, I pull in here as if by a powerful magnet, leaving none at large. Accordingly, it is impossible to pin me down either to my center here or to the centers of my regional observers there.

I am something like a game of hide-and-seek in which hider and seeker never meet because each takes refuge in the other.

Everybody is out on a visit; but because
no one will stay at home to be visited,
there are no meetings. We all keep our
distance by changing places, and
live inside out.

One of the reasons why we can never
meet is that we more than meet: we
become one another.

RESISTANCE

It's strange.
We think we want to see Who we are;
we think we want to be free.

But I perceive a great resistance, largely
because seeing that we are
nothing seems to be the
end of the story.

If we can quickly go on to perceive that as "nothing"
we are also all things, that it's a case of trading one
little guy for the whole world, then we can see
it's very good business.
It's not losing out. Quite the contrary.

Saying Yes! to what happens to me is often
excruciatingly difficult, of course, but it turns out
to be the recipe for the only peace worth having.

I see that right here all my resistance is dissolved
and I'm burst wide open to receive whatever's
in store for me.

So at last the paradox holds:
It's because I have no will that
my will is done.

BEHAVIOR

I find that when I clearly see Who's seeing, it is
unnecessary—it is fatal to that seeing—to worry
about what to say or do, or think or feel: the
fitting expression of First Personhood occurs
as a matter of course, spontaneously,
according to circumstances.
The outcome is unpredictable.

If it proves unconventional, crazy, shocking, or
even wicked by local third-person standards, this
can't be helped. In the long run,
it is what's needed.

I know how to wait,
but cease dithering.

When they are really required,
the right things are done.

So I don't resolve in advance not
to be unloving and mean and petty
and irritable; not to boast, overeat,
steal, flatter, despise, fret, sulk
(the list is endless), though it
may well turn out that such
behavior doesn't occur when
I'm attentive to the Source
of all behavior.

FEELINGS

When people say they don't see it they generally mean
they don't feel it; the inner landscape leaves them cold.

But of course it does! Thank God for that.
This is a matter of fact and not of feeling, of
one's eternal and natureless Nature and not of the
ever-changing kaleidoscope of
thoughts and emotions it
gives rise to.

It's the Truth that sets us free, and
the Truth couldn't be more plain:
plain in the sense of cool and
undecorated; plain in the
sense of
unhidden.

We're always trying to manipulate our feelings.

The only way to do something about our feelings,
perhaps not very much, is to go upstream of
feelings and see Who has them.

So feelings, whether negative or positive, are an
opportunity for seeing Who we are.
It's not symmetry; it's asymmetry.
It's feelings to No-feelings.

The Space I am is not a feeling Space. It's *capacity*
for feeling. My nature always is to be free from
what is filling it. Feelings are up and down. That
makes life interesting. But Who I am Here is
not subject to those variations.

Who I really, really am is my blessing, my refuge.

TIMELESS

Different places have different times, and
when you go there you check what *the time is*
by consulting clocks and watches. To find out
what the time is at Home, you bring your
watch right up to your Eye—only to
discover that here *the time isn't!*

Intrinsically

you are

timeless.

To realize this instantaneous Now, to live in the present moment, taking no thought for tomorrow or yesterday, must be my first concern. And my second must be to find in this Now all my tomorrows and yesterdays.

Seeing Who one is occurs out of time, because seeing Who one is is God seeing Who He is.

SPIRIT

Spirit by itself, the Awareness and the I AM and the Being that *has to be*, that automatically is its sole self from all eternity, is wonderful.

But infinitely more wonderful is the Spirit, the Being that doesn't *have* to be, the Awareness that with no help and for no reason continually arises from Unawareness, from Nothing whatsoever— thereby making that Nothing extremely precious, as well as indispensable.

By virtue of this Nothing, it's not *what* Spirit is but *that* it is which is so breathtakingly adorable. Much the same applies to the arising of our entire Body-Mind (which is none other than the universe), with no help and for no reason, from bare Spirit.

What a universe it is, what incredible richness and variety gush tirelessly from this unutterably simple I AM that I am!

RETURNING

Paradoxically, I'm forever returning to the Place I never left.

And Heaven help me if I kid myself that I've traveled that road often enough, thank you very much, and it's high time I settled down comfortably at the comfortable end of it.

What this means in
practice is that every time
I arrive here is a "first
time"—because in fact
it's out of time.

It means that my
disappearing in your favor
gets more and more
surprising, my single eye
opens wider and wider with
amazement, and I shall
never get used to how my
Renault Clio stirs the
world as if it were a
bowl of porridge.

OBVIOUS

If we would relax into what is blazingly obvious, we
should find all that we need. It is a kind, kind old
world. It hides nothing essential. The more
essential a thing is, the more given it is. We
imagine it's the other way around. What is really
important is given free now.

If I fail to see what I am (and especially what I am
not), it's because I'm too busily imaginative, too
"spiritual," too adult and knowing, too credulous,
too intimidated by society and language, too
frightened of the obvious, to accept the situation
exactly as I find it at this moment.

Only I am in a position to report on what's here.

A kind of alert naivety is what I need. It takes an
innocent eye and an empty head (not to mention a
stout heart) to admit one's own perfect emptiness.

Until you see What you are you don't know what
obviousness is! All else is more or less veiled.
Compared with this Sight, all other
sights are obscure, fuzzy,
groping,
dim.

SIGHT-SEEING

It isn't that I *could* be wrong
about the object out there,
but that to some extent
I *must* be
wrong:
to apprehend
it at all is to
misapprehend it.

And conversely, it isn't that I'm
likely to be right about the bare
Subject here but that I *must* be
right: To see it at all is to see it
perfectly as it was and is and
shall be for ever and ever, exactly
as all its viewers have seen it
and will see it.

Since there is Nothing to see I
cannot see half
of it, nor can I
half see it; this is an all-or-
nothing (all-*and*-Nothing)
discovery that removes
any anxiety lest my
Enlightenment should be
dimmer than yours, less
mature, or deficient in
any way whatsoever.

To see this one perfect Sight
is perfect Sight-seeing;
therefore among those who
enjoy it there can be no
élite, no pecking order—
while the
seeing lasts.

NOT KNOWING

The great secret of life, the great know-how, is *not*
to know, to be at a loss—to be, precisely, at my
wit's end, which is the beginning of the Wit of the
One I really, really am.

Every "choice" that is made from *not* knowing,
from *not* having it all taped, from *not* having it in a
briefcase, from *not* having a script or a rule, but
from the Clarity Here and what fills it, seems to
me to be a whole different deal, the true surrender.

Everything I do is either coming from my human nature, from my "Douglas image" illegitimately and nonsensically superimposed on the Center of my life, or else it is coming from what is at the Center of my life, from Who I am.

The difference between those two kinds of action doesn't look like much, but it is very, very deep.

You could sum up the authentic one as not knowing. **Only don't know.**

UNWORLDLY
VALUES

To the extent that I stay centered in the
perfection of the New Man, of my True
Nature as First Person singular, the
manifold imperfections of the
old man are mitigated.

To the extent that I live from the values of this New Man—unconditional love, no power over others, no turning one's back on them, the acceptance of humiliation, and so forth—to that extent the contrasting values of that old man become less and less heavy and humorless and troublesome, and more and more amenable and realistic and healthy.

In a word, more natural.

Everything I have been brought up to believe about who I really am is upside down and wrong.

FASCINATING

Open
your
Eye
now to
What
you
are,
to
this
Eye
itself.

Are
you
bored
to
tears
with
this,
right
now?

How
could
you
ever
have
too
much
of a
thing
that is
No-
thing?

How could you ever get fed up with this
No-object, which offhandedly pops up
with universes?

Is it not excellent value—this World's End, this
Neckline of yours that sports the whole space-time
world above it but no space and no time and no
world—absolutely damn all—below it?

Only give it half a chance and I guarantee that
you will find that this No-thing is the only thing
you never get sick to the back teeth of, that never
loses its charm, that is always brand new, that
you never, never get used to.

Try it now for sheer breathtaking interest,
dear reader.

NON-MYSTICAL

Unlike ideas and feelings, you can have this simple seeing when you need it most, as when you are agitated or worried. It's ready at hand for dealing with troubles as they arise, on the spot.

This meditation is certainly not in itself a mystical or religious experience, not euphoric, not a sudden expansion into universal love or cosmic consciousness, not any kind of feeling or thought or intuition whatever. Quite the contrary, it is absolutely featureless, colorless, neutral.

It is gazing into the pure, still, cool, Transparent
Fountainhead, and simultaneously out from It at
the streaming, turbulent world—without being
carried away into that world.

You can ensure your full share of mystical or
spiritual experiences, not by going downstream
after them, but only by noticing that you are
forever upstream of them all, and they can
only be enjoyed there from their
Source in you.

I AM YOU

The practical difference this discovery
makes to your relationships is immense
and cumulative. In fact, what it comes
to is that you aren't *related* in any way
to anyone: you *are* that one. In
contrast to the self-regarding and
sentimental and very choosy love
(so-called) much cultivated on Earth,
this is the true love of Heaven, and it
is love of all. Here, undiscriminating
love is one's very Nature.

When I really attend, when I'm honest
with myself, I find it impossible to
wash my hands of the wickedest or
stupidest or most contemptible or
saddest creature in the world.

It is not a case of "There, but for the grace of God, go I" but of "There go I—into the prison cell, into the psychiatric ward, on to the scaffold, no less than happier places"—for the simple but truly devastating reason that Who I really, really am is what you and all others really, really are.

NO RULES

If I'm observed to be living up to any
"principles," this is an incidental and external
view, for the One here is innocent of
principles—and everything else.

Nor is this the
substitution of the
Law of Love for the
Ten Commandments.

The Void here, which is the
Source not only of love
but its opposite, knows no law.

The First Person is inevitably a-moral, a-everything, for to *prescribe rules to* myself is to make a case of myself, to cultivate a face or self-image, to box myself, to become a memory, a third person, a separate thing that is naturally selfish.

Conversely, to *be Myself* is to be this First Person Singular who, as consciously identical with all other First Persons (not that there are such), is naturally "unselfish" and whose "goodness" owes nothing to rules and is truly creative.

NON-VISUAL

Close your eyes . . .

drop memory
and imagination, and notice whether you have
any limits now or are in any kind of box.

AWARENESS

Aren't you more like

room, silence for these

sounds to happen in,

space for these passing

sensations of warmth,

pressure, etc., this flow

of feelings and

thoughts?

Just room or capacity—

but *aware* of itself

now as that!

LOOKING

Stop believing things
and just have a look,
as if for the first time.

This seeing of the Perfect One
at your core is instantaneous
and perfect seeing. There are
no blurred or partial sightings
of your Origin.

How different it is when you view Its products!
Things are too complex and too missing, too
scattered in space and time, too out-to-lunch,
to be seen. At best they are glimpsed.

Range is what matters. Move in toward yourself
and you have a long succession of perishing
appearances. Move all the way in and you are the
Imperishable Reality they are appearances of.

If you want to be Real, you must break the habit of
continually leaping out in the effort to see
yourself as others see you.

**Cultivate the habit of sitting at
Home and see yourself directly.**

PRACTICE

Seeing what you really are is just about
the easiest thing in the world to do, and
just about the most difficult to
keep doing—at first.

Normally, it takes months and years and
decades of coming back home, to the
spot one occupies (or rather, doesn't
occupy—the world does that) before one
learns the knack of remaining centered,
of staying indoors, of living from one's
space instead of from one's face.

Now that you know how to get there,
you can visit home whenever you wish
and whatever your mood. Once over the
threshold, you're perfectly at home.

Here, you can't put a foot wrong.
Practice doesn't make perfect here; it is
perfect from the start. You can't half see
your facelessness now, or see half of it.

There are no degrees of enlightenment:
it is all or nothing.

TWO-WAY
LOOKING

When two-way looking is persisted in, the
external world is much more truly and vividly
seen than when it is viewed by itself as if it were
the whole story, as if it were unobserved.

Even this enlightened way of looking
at the world doesn't begin to perfect
one's knowledge of the world, whose very
nature is that it can only be inspected
piecemeal and never comprehensively.

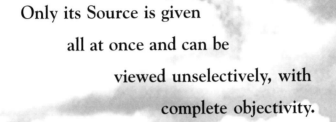

Only its Source is given
all at once and can be
viewed unselectively, with
complete objectivity.

RESULTS

The days of weeks or months following your initial seeing (whether it came explosively or not) are liable to prove joy-filled and lightsome. You feel new-born into a new world. But sooner rather than later, alas, all this fades—much to your surprise and disappointment. "It does nothing for me!"

The temptation is then to give up the meditation, under the mistaken impression that you have lost the art of it. In fact, if you persist nevertheless, it comes to be valued less for its appetizing but incidental fruits than for itself—for the plain and savorless truth of it, for the nothing that it does indeed do for you, instead of the something it used to do—and this is a great advance.

Beginning to lose interest in the fruits, you ensure they grow all the more healthily, unobserved and undisturbed, and ripen in season.

Meantime, and always, your sole business is their nourishing Root.

EVER NEW

One of the paradoxes of the Emptiness here
is how, though forever the same, it gets more
intriguing, more surprising, more wonderful,
more precious, the more it is noticed.

Here, and here alone, familiarity breeds
respect, dedication, reverence.

This isn't a matter of theory but of observation.

The consistent report is that everything—
when taken by itself—sooner or later grows
dull and boring, whereas the No-thing it
comes from never loses its brightness.

Nor is this the end of the story.

The surprisingly happy sequel is this: All these emergent things, so tiresome on their own, when seen in the only way they really can be seen, from the station of their Origin here, are bathed in the glow of that Origin.

They have the refreshing taste of their Source; they smell of their native land, the Country of Everlasting Clearness.

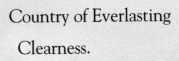

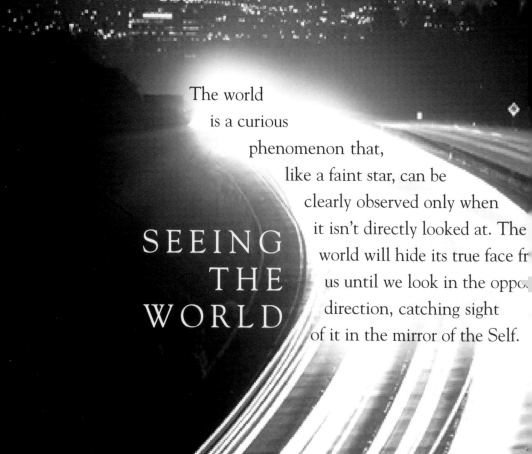

The world
is a curious
phenomenon that,
like a faint star, can be
clearly observed only when
it isn't directly looked at. The
world will hide its true face fr
us until we look in the oppo
direction, catching sight
of it in the mirror of the Self.

SEEING
THE
WORLD

Colors, textures, sounds, tastes, smells—
all sensations are apt to take on a new
brilliance, poignancy, novelty, in the
sharpest contrast to their plain
Background here. For instance, it is
common (even when one has just begun
to see) to find colors—such as the traffic
lights and pavements and the sides of
taxis—unbelievably glowing
and beautiful.

*It's not when you look at but when you
overlook the Seer that the seen
grows dim and distorted.*

Not only the "outer" world, but also your
"inner" world of psychological states is
obscured when you ignore the Inmost
that covers and underlies them all.

CLEAR
VISION

So long as I fabricate here this central obstruction,
this nut of a head, this solid and opaque ball or
blob, to serve as the nucleus of my universe, then I
am not only hard and hard-faced, but also dense
and small-minded; my vision is blocked, my
understanding blurred and
darkened, my world-
picture
distorted.

To be wrongheaded (and to be headed
here *is* to be wrong) about the central
fact of my world is to be wrong about the
rest. Expecting otherwise (as if one could
be sane outside and mad inside) is like
expecting a watch to go without its
mainspring, a tree to flourish without its
root, a lamp to shine without
wick or oil.

How odd that the one spot in the
universe that I had systematically
overlooked turns out to be the Spot that
matters, the more-than-holy Ground
that is, precisely, the Solution of all
problems and the Fountainhead
of all creation!

My mirror is a marvelous, marvelous
teacher, more valuable than all
the scriptures of the world.

My mirror confirms this wide-openness right
here where I am. The very thing that long ago
put a face on me now relieves me of it. Now I
look in the glass to see what I'm not like!

The whole of my life and what I have to share with people is "Come back from identifying with the guy in the mirror, who is very important but is *there*. Come back from him there to *here*, to his Origin, which is exactly where you are."

THE MIRROR

Everything perishes.
If you don't want to perish,
go where there isn't
anything to perish.
Then you find that
you are already there.

Seeing is the
profoundest
kind of dying.

Here, you are deader than
dead. Not until you see this
clearly and accept it deeply are you
empty enough, are you burst wide
open enough, to be flooded with the
resurrection life that is the life of the
whole world. When you find, beyond all
doubt, that you are this dreadful Waste Land,
then you find there the Holy Grail, already
flooding you to overflowing with its living water.

DEATH

RESURRECTION

To live is to be the resurrection
and the life of others.

Where I'm coming from is upstream of life.
It is the source of life, yes, but it is not
alive. From Here I look out upon a snail
or the daffodil there, let alone you,
and, my God, I discover life.

It's the old, old story: die to live.
Give your life.
The way to have your life is to
give it up, dying into the new life.

In the Whole all the
dead wholly live, and
in the Center all the
living wholly die.

Here, we lose ourselves and
find Ourself in a deathless world
whose divisions and opacity
have finally vanished, and
where everything is
indescribably weightless
and open and brilliant.

WASHOUT

It is a marvelous thing to realize that as human beings we are a washout, that everything is lost, that the whole situation has gone to pot.

Then we rely only on Who we are.

We have to die
before God
can live in us.

GRACE

We discover at our heart the power
and the glory behind the world.

This is the message of Christianity and of all the great religions: that at your heart is the kingdom and the power and the glory.

It's not because you deserve it. It's grace.

Far from deserving it,
on the contrary,
it's a free gift,
begging to be noticed.

NO METHOD

We do too much and therefore remain ineffectual,
we talk far too much and therefore say nothing,
we think far, far too much and therefore prevent
the facts from
speaking for
themselves—so
say those who
know the
value of
emptiness.

It's for us to make our own
tests, not—repeat *not*—by
the direct method of trying to
be quiet and mindless (it just
won't work) but by the
indirect method of seeing
Who, it seems, was trying
to be like that.

No man becomes Godlike except
by seeing that he isn't a
man anyway.

SAFE
HAVEN

So it all comes
back to the crucial
question of my
true Identity.

If I insist on making
an object, a thing
and a third person of
myself here, I am
consumed with a
thousand fears and
better off dead.

But if I give up this unrealistic and unrewarding habit and come to Myself, I see that I have never emerged from that marvelous Abyss, that before Abraham was I am, before the first galaxy and the first atom, before time itself.

Right here and now, in the very place all this stormy weather of time and change come from, I am Home and dry.

Where can I go from this Safe Haven?

IMPERISHABLE

There are all sorts of advantages of
being No-thing, of being Space really,
because things are at risk, are up
against one another; they are threats
to one another. Each is asserting itself,
crowding others out of its space.

Things exclude one another.

That may have certain attractions,
but it certainly makes you, if you are a
thing, terribly at risk, and basically
frightened, because things perish.

You should be frightened
because things perish.

If you are No-thing, it raises the
question of whether you can
perish at all.

If you are Space/Awareness, is
that the kind of thing that
perishes, that comes
and goes?

SAFETY

What a relief to be backed by the One whose
name is I AM, the name that precedes and
introduces every other name.

What a relief to merge into and be
upheld by the Unlimited.

This meditation is safe, not only because it can't
be bungled, not only because it avoids dependence
upon others on the one hand, and self-pride on
the other, but also because it is uncontrived.
There's nothing arbitrary or fanciful about it,
nothing to strain your credulity, nothing to go
wrong, nothing to set you apart from
ordinary people, nothing special.

It is safe because it is finding out how matters
stand, not trying to manipulate them.

What could be less dangerous than
ceasing to deceive yourself
about your Self, or more
dangerous than
not doing
so?

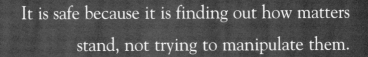

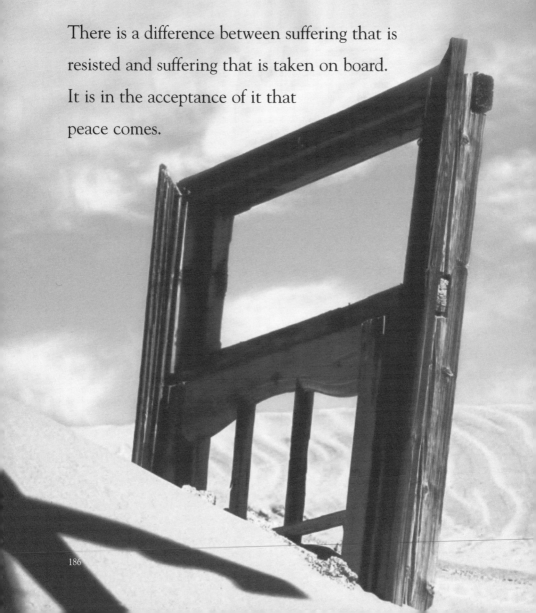

Total acceptance is very hard.
It's precisely the opposite of the
lazy indifference that lets things slide.
It springs from inner strength and not weakness,
from concentration, not slackness.

There is a difference between suffering that is
resisted and suffering that is taken on board.
It is in the acceptance of it that
peace comes.

ACCEPTANCE

Why is the world so troublesome,
so frightful?

Is it like that by nature, or because we take the
easy way of fighting it instead of the difficult
way of fitting in with it? We have to find out
for ourselves the truth of the sage's
demonstration that even in the smallest things
the way of noninterference, of giving up all
self-will, of "disappearing," is astonishingly
practical, the way that works.

Not only in the long run but from moment to
moment, consciously getting out of the Light,
giving place to whatever happens to be
presenting itself in that Light, is
astonishingly creative.

TRUST

The more steadily I gaze at the One that's nearest
and clearest, the more it turns out to be the
dearest, more me than myself, the Resource
that never *really* lets me down.

The Wide-Awake One that—though homely and
obvious and transparent through and through—
fills me with worship and wonder at the mystery of
its self-origination. Who shall set limits to the
bright blessings that can arise from our growing
willingness to trust what we see, instead of
what we're told to see?

Things can't be trusted. They pose problems, they change, they perish. Not so this Aware No-thing. It alone can be relied on. It comes up with things—not, it's true, with the things you imagine you want, but with the things you really, really want, the things you need. Is this so surprising?

After all, it's from this same unspeakably mysterious No-thing that *all* things emerge for no reason (why should they?), that this wildly improbable universe is now emerging.

SURRENDER

If all we want is to see Who we really, really are,
nothing can stop us from doing so this
very moment.

But if our plan is to use that blessed vision to buy
baskets full of nice feelings or any other goodies,
we might as well abandon the very idea
of Self-inquiry.

So long as any part of me remains
unsurrendered, I shall
never be Myself.

Until the will is surrendered,
there is no
peace.

PEACE

If I am perfectly contented now, it is because I
have ceased to be any kind of Container at all,
but instead am con*tent* with my *cont*ent.

Peace is our very nature, not something we come
across. It's where we are, nearer than all else.
We don't come to it; we come from it.
To find it is to allow ourselves
to go back to the place
we never left.

**At the Center
is always
perfection . . .**

**. . . off-Center is
always imperfection.**

One thing alone can be relied on through all
circumstances, and that is their Core of Peace.
The seer may often find himself in a tragic and sad
and puzzling and troublesome world, but he never
(so long as he's seeing) lacks peace of mind.
His basic anxiety has gone.

Seeing that he is indeed Peace Itself, he is at rest.

TEN
EXPERIMENTS

POINTING

Point at the wall ahead. See how solid and opaque it is.

Slowly bring your finger down until it is pointing at the floor. You are still pointing at something, a surface.

Next, bring your hand round and point to your feet . . . your legs . . . your trunk . . . your chest—also somethings, also surfaces.

Point to what is above your chest: to your neck, your face, your eyes . . . Or rather, to the place where people told you those things are to be found.

YOU ARE NOW POINTING AT NO SURFACE, AT NO THING AT ALL.

Check that it is featureless, colorless, transparent, boundless. Keep on pointing, seeing into emptiness; see how wide, how deep, how high is this no-thing that is on your side of that in-pointing finger.

And see how, just because it is so empty *of* everything, it is empty *for* everything. See how full it is of the whole colorful and changing scene—of the ceiling, the walls, the window, and the view from it; the floor, those legs and that trunk, and that pointing finger itself. See how the no-thing that you are *is* all the things that are on show.

Have you ever been other than this NO-THING/ALL THINGS?

OPENING YOUR TRUE (THIRD) EYE

You can see that a human being has *two* "windows" in a head. And, he will tell you he's looking at you through his *eyes* (in the plural)—his *two eyes* or *a pair of eyes*—not his eye.

The question is: What are *you* looking out of right now, in your own firsthand experience? Are you taking in these letters and words—these rows of black marks on white paper—through *two* tiny peepholes?

Or are you taking them in through *one* very large and very clear "picture window"—so large it has no frame or definite boundaries at all, and so clear it's as if it were unglazed and stood wide, wide open?

In fact, is anything whatever to be found now on your side—the near side—of the scene? Or have you vanished in its favor, become mere Capacity, empty for these pages, for the hands and truncated arms holding them, and their blurred background?

SEEING YOUR TRUE (ORIGINAL) FACE

Human beings confront the world, are up against it, find themselves face-to-face with others like themselves. That's the way they talk, the way they look, the way they are.

Do *you* relate to people that way? Do *you* face them, confront them?

Turn to someone in the room, or to your own face in the mirror, or just examine the face pictured here. See whether you have anything where you are to match that shape and those colors, that opacity and those textures, any features whatever—let alone ones capable of getting in the way of the scene, of changing their expression, of aging.

Isn't your own real "Face" like an absolutely blank screen, or unpainted canvas, or glassless mirror, ever ready to take on and instantly discard without trace an endless succession of human and animal faces? Isn't it ever ready to become each face and each scene in turn, with astonishing brilliance and in minutest detail?

Has your own "Face" ever had any complexion or features of its own that could be born as an infant's face and grow up into an adult's face—let alone wrinkle, and die, and decay?

YOUR TWO FACES

If you haven't got an oval or round hand mirror, an ordinary rectangular one will do. Hold out the mirror, find your face in it, and keep it there throughout the experiment.

Dropping belief and imagination, see where that face presents itself. Notice the place where you keep it: at the *far* end of your arm.

This is where others, too, pick it up. This is where they hold their cameras to photograph it and where you put your camera to make a self-portrait. It has never been much nearer to you than that, or much farther away.

Moreover, you can now see that that thing is not, and has never been, at the *near* end of your arm, mounted on *these* shoulders.

There, a meter or so away, is your human face, your acquired face, your appearance. It is a thing. *Here*, right here, is your non-human Face, your Original Face, your Reality. It is not a thing. See now how great the contrast is between them. See how spotlessly clear and unlined the complexion of this one is, how wide open and serene its expression, how relaxed. And, yes, how beautiful! And that little, closed-up face over there? Well, that's for the people around to cope with.

CLOSED EYE
EXPERIMENT

Ask a friend to read you the following questions while you keep your eyes closed.

- On present evidence, what are you like now?
- How many legs, arms, heads, bodies—if any—can you detect?
- How big are you?
- Can you truly say, "I am this or that?"
- Can you not nevertheless say, "I AM"?
- Is your sense of BEING any less strong now than when you see or think of yourself as something or other? Is it, perhaps, much stronger now?
- Is it dependent on any of your senses?
- Has this I-AM-ness any features that could link it with your human aspect or anything else at all; or that could separate it from I-AM-ness, however or wherever or whenever enjoyed?
- Being thus at your own Center, aren't you also at the Center of all beings, of all BEING, and much nearer to them than their own hands and feet? And much nearer to me than these hands and feet of mine?

DISCOVERING YOU ARE FOREVER STILL

People move around and are very happy to do so. They will tell you how much they resent and dread getting stuck. In fact, all bodies are mobile: living bodies particularly so, weaving ever-changing patterns of great complexity.

If you are not the body-thing, but instead are the boundless No-thing or Space which contains it—along with all the other things—don't you have to be absolutely immobile? Surely a boundless No-thing on the move is nonsense, impossible.

Well, let's *see*. I'm asking you to test yourself for mobility-immobility right away. Please stand up, and, while pointing to what you're looking out of—your "face"—notice how in fact that finger is pointing at No-thing at all. Then, while continuing to look simultaneously out at the finger-thing there and in at the No-thing here, start rotating on the spot. And notice how in fact it's not you but the room that's rotating. Fifteen seconds will be enough, then slow the room down, stop it turning, and sit down again. It's so easy a task, taking up so little time, that I must respectfully insist that you don't merely read about it, but do what I ask you, now.

Wasn't it indeed the room—the ceiling, walls, windows, pictures—that went round and round, and weren't you the still Space they went round in?

Next time you consider moving down a corridor, check how impossible it is for you—the real you, the First Person—to do so, and how instead it moves down you, and is swallowed up in your immensity-immobility.

When you next drive your car, check that it's the whole scene that's in motion—things in the far distance, such as hills, very slowly; things in the middle distance, such as houses, more quickly; near things, such as telegraph poles and lamp-posts, very swiftly indeed—in a grand procession through your stillness. You may notice that you have no way and no need to *go* anywhere, seeing that all the things and places ahead—road-side buildings, villages, towns, countries—are obligingly coming to you and pouring themselves into you; and no way and no need to *leave* anywhere, seeing that those same things and places (as you can see in your rear-view mirror) are pouring themselves out of you and obligingly retreating into the distance. And all the while you don't budge an inch! How magnificently you are served!

DISCOVERING YOU ARE TIMELESS • PART 1

Whether alive or not, things invariably take time to be what they are. Thus an atom isn't an atom until its electrons are given long enough to sweep out their orbits. Thus a human being isn't a human being until he or she has had time to progress through and incorporate many drastic transformations, in the course of his or her history as an embryo and fetus, and then as an infant and child. None of this amazing past is wiped out by the present. A notable time-binder, a human includes his or her entire history, and acts now with all that history at his or her back.

Now if, in total contrast to your peripheral human nature, your own true and fundamental Nature—what you are at center, in and for yourself—is indeed just Empty Space or Bare Capacity or Absolute Stillness, then you need no time at all to be yourself; you bind or incorporate no time whatever. Having nothing here to body forth or build up or maintain, presumably you have here no use for time, and accordingly are timeless. As always, let's *see*.

Not only are things out there—unlike you, presumably—compounded of time, but they are arranged in time-zones according to their distances from you. Your wristwatch indicates that, a foot or so away such and such is the time there. And you have good reasons for supposing that in New York and Tokyo and other places the local timepieces are registering other times.

Now the question is: What time is it exactly where you are, at the center of all these time zones?

You find out in the normal way, by consulting the local timepieces, in the absence of which your own wristwatch will do very well.

Having read off the time it shows a foot away, very slowly and attentively bring it toward you while continuing to read off the time, until it will come no nearer. Isn't it the case that those printed numerals soon blur, then become illegible, and in the end disappear altogether? That, in fact, your central time zone turns out to be timeless? That time, forever eccentric, can never get Home to *you*? That whereas you contain time along with the world it builds, it can never contain you? That the Law of Asymmetry applies here as always, and (just as it's face there to no-face here, color there to no-color here, and so on) it's time there to no-time here. Naturally so, seeing that as First Person you are no-thing and where there's no-thing there's no change, and where there's no change there's no way of registering time, and where there's no way of registering time there's no time.

Again, since the issue is precisely a life-or-death one, I must ask you to overcome your reluctance to conduct so "unnecessary," so "silly" and "childish" an experiment. Isn't it possible—even probable—that until you become like a little child (as unembarrassed and guileless and unopinionated as that, as seriously playful as that) you will never enter the Kingdom, will never leave the time-ruled realm of death for the deathless realm?

DISCOVERING YOU ARE TIMELESS • *PART 2*

The following test applies more particularly to those of us who have been looking into our No-thingness for some time. Nevertheless new Seers are encouraged to have a go. In fact, this distinction between us "old hands" at the job and you "new ones" is provisional: we're about to discover if there's anything in it.

While pointing in once more, examine carefully this very odd place you're pointing at . . . Are you now gazing timelessly into the infinite depths of your timeless Origin and Destiny, into the abyss of your changeless and deathless Nature . . . ? Could this be nothing less than the Eternal contemplation of Eternity…?

To check whether, simply by turning your attention through 180°, you at once enter a world where temporal distinctions no longer apply, please answer as many of the following questions as you can:

- Are you able to put a date and time—by the clock—on your first seeing into your No-thingness? Are you sure there was a first time?
- Maybe you can remember the circumstances of many an occasion of in-seeing—the encounters and ideas that led up to it, the setting, the feelings and behavior it gave rise to—but can you remember the seeing itself and what it was you saw? Does memory have any access here?
- Does it mean anything to talk about long or short intervals, or any gaps whatever, between one in-seeing and the next? Does it make sense to speak of a long and sustained in-seeing (lasting, say, three days, or an hour

and a quarter, or six minutes) in contrast to a brief one (lasting, say, 3.85 seconds)? Or to refer to plural in-seeings at all?

- Do you catch yourself distinguishing between a good day when your in-seeing is well-maintained, an average day when it's often interrupted, and a bad day when it's only occasional? Can in-seeing be measured in these terms— in any terms?
- Do you ever feel—you "long-time and practiced in-seers"—at an advantage, or superior to "novice in-seers"?

Insofar as your answer to these questions is NO!, here's more evidence that your in-seeing is nothing less than the Eternal seeing into Eternity. But *of course*, in that case, it has no time for clocks and calendars and diaries; but *of course* it's hopelessly vague about what happened when; but *of course* it telescopes time; but *of course* it fails to distinguish between beginners and past masters at the job! One of those masters being John Tauler, who wrote: "A man who really and truly enters his Ground feels as though he has been there throughout Eternity." Isn't all this just what you'd expect of a 180° turnabout from time to the Timeless?

And the practical upshot of this test?

What an instant resource, as awesome as it is intimate and as mysterious as it is available, we have right here! What a medicine against death, what an everlasting refuge, lies at our very heart, visibly expanding to take in and take care of everything! And given NOW in its fullness and depth— however incompetent or undeserving we may be, whatever our mood and just when we need it most!

HAVING AN OUT-OF-THE-BODY EXPERIENCE

People coincide with their bodies. They are stationed inside and not outside them. As if to assure you of this, they speak of their "sojourn in this house of clay," or their "present incarnation," or even their "imprisonment in the flesh." And many add that when they die they will be released from this body and take up residence elsewhere—for instance in a new sort of "spiritual body" in Heaven or Purgatory or Hell, or in another physical body on Earth.

Does any of this apply to you—to the real you of the present moment? In other words, are you shut up in anything whatever? Are you small, restricted, embodied?

Look at that hand. Are you *inside* that object? If so, tell me what it's like in there! Small, congested, dark, wet? Can you begin to describe—not from hearsay or memory or guesswork—its bone and muscle structure, its veins and arteries and nerve fibers?

Instead of your being *in it*, isn't it *in you*? I refer to the look of it, the feel of it, the use of it.

People talk of rare and wonderful out-of-the-body experiences. Have you ever had any other sort, any *in-the-body* experiences—except in imagination?

It's reported that a typical component of the so-called Near Death Experience is *looking down on your body from above*. Why wait till your deathbed for that moment of truth? Why not make *this* moment the moment of truth? Move this book to one side and look down *now* at that trunk, at those arms and legs. Look down from on high, not out of two eyes in a head, but out of empty and unbounded Space: Look down from what you can now see is an indeterminate distance above that decapitated form—a distance that reaches far beyond—yet embraces—that form.

Aren't you already loose, and free-ranging, and at large, no more confined to that body than to this page, those shoes, that carpet? Have you ever *not* been like this?

Could this be the true, the ever-present rising from the tomb, the resurrection into undying life—right now?

FINGER PRESSING

Hold out your hand and press your forefinger against your thumb as hard as you can…

Notice where the stress is, on present evidence—namely, in those things. And notice where the absence of stress is—namely, in yourself as the no-thing that is taking in those things, along with their shape and color and opacity. Notice how *you* are no more stressed by the stress in that hand than you are shaped by the shape of that hand, or colored by the color of that hand, or clouded by that hand's opacity. As empty for all things of their qualities and their stresses, you just can't help being different from all that. It is your essential nature to remain unaffected, as unstained and uninjured and unstressed as your TV screen is by all the murders and shootings and burnings that rage on it—as unsoiled as your mirror is by what it mirrors so faithfully and so unselectively.

BIBLIOGRAPHY

Face to No-Face

Fate and Freedom (article)

Head Off Stress

Interview (conducted by Richard Lang in 1977)

The Life and Philosophy of Douglas Harding (video)

Look For Yourself

Melbourne Lecture (video)

On Having No Head

On Having No Head (video)

Seeing Who You Really Are (by Richard Lang)

The Headless Way

The Hierarchy of Heaven and Earth

The Trial of the Man Who Said He Was God

Yellow Toolkit

The Little Book of Life and Death

The Science of the 1st Person

To Be and Not To Be

Toolkit for Testing the Incredible Hypothesis (out of print)

The Middle Way: Journal of the Buddhist Society (1963 Article "Thirty Questions")

ABOUT THE EDITOR

Richard Lang is Coordinator of The Shollond Trust, a UK charity (1059551) set up to help make the Headless Way more available. He also teaches Tai Chi and 5 Rhythms Dance and practices as a psychotherapist. His book, *Seeing Who You Really Are*, was published in 2003. He travels widely giving workshops on the Headless Way.

For more information on the Headless Way, visit:
www.headless.org or email Richard Lang at
headexchange@gn.apc.org

ABOUT INNER DIRECTIONS

Inner Directions is the imprint of the Inner Directions Foundation, a nonprofit organization dedicated to exploring self-discovery and awakening to one's essential nature.

We publish distinctive books, videos, and audiotapes that express the heart of authentic spirituality. Each of our titles presents an original perspective, with a clarity and insight that can only come from the experience of ultimate reality. These unique publications communicate the immediacy of *That* which is eternal and infinite within us: the nondualistic ground from which religions and spiritual traditions arise.

If you recognize the merit of an organization whose sole purpose is to disseminate works of enduring spiritual value, please consider becoming a financial supporter. To find out how you can help sponsor an upcoming publishing project, or to request a copy of the *Inner Directions Journal/Catalog*, call, write, or e-mail:

Inner Directions
P. O. Box 130070
Carlsbad, CA 92013

Tel: 760 599-4075
Fax: 760 599-4076
Orders: 800 545-9118

E-mail: mail@InnerDirections.org
Website: www.InnerDirections.org